POACHING

20 NEW WAYS WITH A TRADITIONAL SKILL

LIGHT AND HEALTHY EATING WITH A DIFFERENCE: A DELICIOUS CLASSIC COOKING TECHNIQUE THAT TRAPS
THE FULL FLAVOUR OF FOOD • 20 SAVOURY AND SWEET RECIPES SHOWN IN 100 BEAUTIFUL PHOTOGRAPHS

EDITED BY BRIDGET JONES

This edition is published by Lorenz Books, an imprint of Anness Publishing Ltd, Hermes House, 88–89 Blackfriars Road, London SE1 8HA
tel. 020 7401 2077; fax 020 7633 9499

www.lorenzbooks.com; www.annesspublishing.com

If you like the images in this book and would like to investigate using them for publishing, promotions or advertising, please visit our website www.practicalpictures.com for more information.

UK agent: The Manning Partnership Ltd;
tel. 01225 478444; fax 01225 478440; sales@manning-partnership.co.uk
UK distributor: Grantham Book Services Ltd;
tel. 01476 541080; fax 01476 541061; orders@gbs.tbs-ltd.co.uk
North American agent/distributor: National Book Network;
tel. 301 459 3366; fax 301 429 5746; www.nbnbooks.com
Australian agent/distributor: Pan Macmillan Australia;
tel. 1300 135 113; fax 1300 135 103; customer.service@macmillan.com.au
New Zealand agent/distributor: David Bateman Ltd;
tel. (09) 415 7664; fax (09) 415 8892

PUBLISHER: Joanna Lorenz
MANAGING EDITOR: Linda Fraser
EDITOR: Sarah Uttridge
DESIGNER: Adelle Morris
PRODUCTION CONTROLLER: Claire Rae
RECIPES: Alex Barker, Christine France, Yasuko Fukuoka, Becky Johnson, Kathy Man, Sunil Vijayakar
PHOTOGRAPHY: Steve Baxter, Julie Beresford, Nicki Dowey, Amanda Heywood, William Lingwood

ETHICAL TRADING POLICY
Because of our ongoing ecological investment programme, you, as our customer, can have the pleasure and reassurance of knowing that a tree is being cultivated on your behalf to naturally replace the materials used to make the book you are holding. For further information about this scheme, go to www.annesspublishing.com/trees

A CIP catalogue record for this book is available from the British Library.

Previously published as *Poached*

Main front cover image shows Roasted Garlic and Aubergine Custards with Red Pepper – for recipe, see page 41

NOTES
Bracketed terms are intended for American readers.

For all recipes, quantities are given in both metric and imperial measures and, where appropriate, measures are also given in standard cups and spoons. Follow one set, but not a mixture, because they are not interchangeable.

Standard spoon and cup measures are level.
1 tsp = 5ml, 1 tbsp = 15ml, 1 cup = 250ml/8fl oz

Australian standard tablespoons are 20ml. Australian readers should use 3 tsp in place of 1 tbsp for measuring small quantities of gelatine, flour, salt, etc.

American pints are 16fl oz/2 cups. American readers should use 20fl oz/2.5 cups in place of 1 pint when measuring liquids.

Medium (US large) eggs are used unless otherwise stated.

BREAKFASTS AND BRUNCHES

SOUPS AND LIGHT MEALS

MAIN MEALS

DESSERTS

CONTENTS

gently poached

Poaching is the most relaxed of cooking methods – it merely coaxes ingredients from raw to perfectly cooked. Whereas boiling is rapid, and simmering steady, poaching is a gentle process that makes the most of tender textures and subtle flavours. The food is cooked in liquid just below simmering point. Fragile fish will not fall apart; poultry becomes succulent; eggs are firm; and fruit retains its elusive fragrance. The poaching liquid is the ideal medium for marrying flavouring ingredients with food, for enhancing but not overpowering dishes, so that delicate results are far from dull.

GOOD AND LIGHT

Poaching is a moist cooking method that uses little or no additional fat. It is an extremely healthy way to cook and is especially helpful to anyone who wants to keep their fat intake under control. Without any pre-frying, the ingredients may be heated gently in the liquid from cold or added to barely simmering liquid. The cooked food can be served immediately, or cooled in the liquid, or drained and cooled before being served. Whichever way, the food is always light and moist.

BAGELS

FILLETS OF TURBOT WITH OYSTERS

CHOCOLATE CREPES

FAST AND FABULOUS

Cooking times vary according to the ingredients. While large items, such as whole fish or poultry, take a while to cook, there is a wide range of foods that cook very quickly. Favourites include eggs, fish, finely cut tender poultry or meat, mushrooms, tender leaves and short asparagus tips.

Fabulous flavours are achieved by spiking the cooking liquor and/or dressing, or by seasoning the cooked food before serving. Aromatics, such as vegetables, citrus rind, garlic, herbs and spices, may be used to marinate the food or they may be simmered in the cooking liquor. The emphasis is on complementing the intrinsic flavours within a food or dish rather than enriching by adding the caramel tones that result from frying, roasting or grilling (broiling).

INTERNATIONAL APPEAL

This moist cooking method is used all over the world to infuse ingredients with aromatics. The choice of liquid, seasoning and flavouring varies depending on the ingredients and the type of dish.

Poaching is often taken for granted, but it offers surprising scope. For example, the French poach mousse-like dumplings of fish or poultry, known as quenelle, before serving them in slightly piquant or cream sauces. Flimsy French meringues are poached in milk that is then used as the base for vanilla custard in a light-as-air dessert known as floating islands. Eastern European cooking is renowned for its fabulous dumplings that are light and quite fluffy in texture, with full-flavoured savoury or sweet fillings.

Poaching is sometimes used to pre-cook foods that are then finished by

another method. For example, bratwurst (the smooth-textured German sausages) are poached before being grilled or fried; and bagels – the popular ring-shaped buns – are poached after proving and before baking.

In Japanese recipes, poaching is a popular method for cooking seafood, meat, poultry and tofu, which are often combined with vegetables. Shabu Shabu is a classic Japanese dish of thinly sliced beef and vegetables cooked in stock. The Chinese Mongolian firepot meal is similar, and the poaching stock is thinned and served at the end of the meal as soup.

The following chapters include dishes from all these culinary cultures, with examples of classic ways to poach eggs, Japanese-style beef, and irresistible sweets, including delicate custards and delicious poached fruit.

equipment

FISH KETTLE

EGG POACHER

EGG CODDLERS

Specialist equipment is not necessary for the majority of poaching. As with any cooking method, selecting the most suitable pan for the type of food helps to ensure success. Food can be poached in the oven, in which case an ovenproof dish (with a lid or covered with foil) can be used. Small or large slotted spoons, a fish slice or spatulas are used for adding food to cooking liquid and for lifting it out. When poaching in a shallow volume of liquid, a large spoon is used to baste the food so that it cooks evenly.

FISH KETTLES

These are specialist pans, which are made in an extra-long size to hold large whole fish, typically salmon. They are also made in an off-diamond shape for fish such as whole turbot. Inside the pan, there is a perforated rack on short legs to keep it off the pan base, with handles for easy removal. The rack is used to lower the fish into the poaching liquid and to remove it later.

EGG POACHERS

Shallow, lidded pans containing small cups held in a stand are known as egg poachers. Strictly speaking, eggs cooked this way are not poached, but steamed, because they do not come in direct contact with the water.

Egg poachers are practical, especially for cooking four eggs simultaneously. The cheapest pans of poor-quality materials are best avoided, because the edge of the egg white cooks too quickly and sticks to the metal container. A fairly heavy pan with thick, non-stick cups gives better results. The cups must be greased with a little butter or oil (olive oil gives a good flavour).

EGG CODDLERS

Coddled eggs are cooked in barely simmering water. They are, essentially, poached rather than boiled, which ensures that the white of the eggs remains tender.

An egg coddler is a small, lidded cooking container into which the egg is broken. The covered container is placed in a pan of gently simmering water. The coddler must be greased with butter or oil.

EGG RINGS

Metal rings primarily intended for keeping eggs in shape during frying can be placed in a pan of water and the eggs broken into them so that they stay in place during poaching. The rings must be greased with a little oil to prevent the eggs from sticking.

SKILLETS, FRYING AND SAUTE PANS

These pans are ideal for poaching fish steaks and fillets, small whole fish (trout, red mullet or mackerel), eggs and other modest portions of light foods. The pan must be deep enough to hold sufficient liquid to poach the food. Lidded pans, often known as skillets, are ideal, especially those with glass lids.

SAUCEPANS AND STOCKPOTS

Large, deep pans are used for poaching slightly denser foods that require a greater depth and volume of liquid. Dumplings sink at first and then rise to the surface as they are cooked. They need a good volume of water so that they do not stick together. A large cut of meat such as salt (corned) beef or silverside (pot roast),or a whole chicken can be poached in a stockpot, allowing plenty of room for vegetables and aromatics, and for the main food to be well covered in liquid.

ROASTING PANS

A fairly deep, heavy roasting pan can be useful for poaching medium-sized fish if you do not own a fish kettle.

Lowering the fish into the pan on a double-thick band of foil allows it to be removed easily once cooking is completed. This method is also useful for poaching dishes such as a ballotine of chicken (a boned bird, which is filled with stuffing and rolled, and is then wrapped in muslin (cheesecloth) and poached gently).

A bain-marie can be used to "poach" a dish of very delicate food, in hot water that is not quite boiling; for example, custard can be poached in this way. Alternatively, a roasting pan can be used as a bain-marie, either on top of the stove or in the oven. Foil can be used to cover a roasting pan, if necessary.

EGG RINGS

STOCKPOT

BAIN-MARIE

perfect poaching

Poaching can be a simple one-step process, where ingredients are added to cold liquid and brought to a simmer, or added to just-simmering liquid. At its most complex, poaching involves no more than three simple stages.

PREPARING THE COOKING LIQUID

Aromatics and seasonings are often simmered in the cooking liquid before adding the food, particularly when poaching ingredients that cook quickly. Ingredients to simmer in the liquid first include onion, garlic, carrot, celery or fennel; bay leaves, parsley, thyme, tarragon or bouquet garni; or spices, such as fresh root ginger, chillies, cinnamon stick, cloves, peppercorns or coriander seeds. Add these to the liquid, bring to the boil, then cover and simmer gently. The liquid may be used immediately or cooled first; it may be strained or the aromatics retained during poaching, depending on the recipe.

Generally, there should be enough liquid to cover the food. Some items are poached in a large volume of liquid, others in very small amounts (in which case they are basted or turned).

POACHING THE FOOD

If the food is heated in cold liquid, avoid heating the liquid too rapidly or to too high a temperature in the first place. Heat gently until the liquid is barely bubbling. The liquid should not boil. If it does so it may toughen the food or cause it to disintegrate.

If a recipe states that food should be added to hot liquid, bring the liquid to a steady stage of barely simmering before adding the food. Control the heat when the food is added to keep the liquid just about simmering, but do not increase it so much that the liquid boils.

Gently spoon liquid over the food for even cooking. Use a spoon and fork, two spoons, a slotted spoon or spatula to turn food if necessary during cooking.

DRAINING AND SERVING

Delicate poached foods are lifted out of the cooking liquor on to a warm plate or dish, using a slotted spoon or spatula. The food may be transferred to a colander for further draining, or on to kitchen paper to absorb any

AROMATICS AND SEASONINGS

POACHING FISH

POACHING EGGS

POACHING SAUSAGES

SHAPING MERINGUES

POACHING FRUIT

unnecessary moisture. Food that needs to be kept hot should be placed in a dish and covered tightly with foil or a tight-fitting lid. The dish should be placed over a pan of hot, not simmering, water (making sure that the dish is not touching the water) to prevent any further cooking.

Some cooking liquids may be reduced by boiling, or they may be strained, seasoned, thickened or enriched to make a sauce, depending on the recipe.

Food may be cooled in the cooking liquor so that it remains moist and succulent. Remove the pan from the heat – it is important that the food does not continue to cook in the hot liquid.

POACHING TIPS

Poaching Eggs Adding 15 ml/1 tbsp vinegar to a shallow pan of barely simmering water helps the white to set

quickly in shape. Swirl the water and slide the egg off a saucer into the swirl for a neat shape. Spoon the edges of the egg inwards during the 1–2 minutes cooking. Drain and trim the edges.

Quenelle Shapes To shape mousse-like mixtures and meringues, you will need to use two spoons. Scoop a portion of mixture, then shape it into a neat oval by scooping from one spoon to the other two or three times. The final "scoop" should be placed into the cooking liquor.

Poaching Whole Fish Tie string around a large whole fish – such as salmon – in two or three places to keep it in a neat shape during cooking.

Poaching Sausages When poaching sausages, such as frankfurters or bratwurst, it is imperative that the water is not even bubbling, otherwise they could burst.

POACHING LIQUIDS

Water Add seasoning, herbs and aromatics. Discard or use as stock.
Stock Good for short cooking times and as a sauce or served as a broth.
Court–Bouillon Water, carrot, onion, celery, peppercorns, bay leaves and white wine vinegar (100ml/4fl oz/$\frac{1}{2}$ cup to 1.1 litres/2 pints/5 cups water) simmered for 15 minutes. Used for poaching fish and discarded after use.
Wine Red or white, used alone or with water as above.
Milk For savoury or sweet dishes. Boil then reduce the heat to a simmer and poach for the recommended time.
Syrup Light syrup for poaching fruit.
Fruit Juice For poaching fruit, meringues or sweet dumplings.

BREAKFASTS
AND BRUNCHES

Classic dishes are always the best choice to get the day off to a good start. Fruit compote, irresistible bagels and poached eggs are on the menu in this chapter, providing a choice of light eating for super-healthy mornings or a good and hearty brunch.

hot fruit compote

Ingredients | SERVES 8

450g|1lb|2¹/₂ cups mixed dried fruit, such as apricots, apples, prunes, sultanas (golden raisins), figs and pears

475ml|16fl oz|2 cups water

thinly pared rind of 1 small lemon or 30ml|2 tbsp lemon juice

1 cinnamon stick

natural (plain) yogurt, to serve

Dried fruits lend themselves to poaching and they retain their shape, texture and flavour beautifully. Serve the compote in small quantities along with a generous dollop of natural yogurt.

1 Unless the fruit is of the ready-to-eat variety, soak overnight in water, then drain, reserving the liquid and transferring it to a medium-sized pan.

2 Make up the liquid to 475ml|16fl oz| 2 cups with water. Add the lemon rind or juice and the cinnamon stick.

3 Bring to the boil, lower the heat then add the drained fruit. Poach for 15 minutes until the fruit is tender. Drain, reserving the syrup, and transfer to individual serving bowls.

4 Return the syrup to the pan and simmer for about 20 minutes until it has reduced slightly and thickened. Pour it over the fruit, and serve warm or cold, with yogurt.

COOK'S TIP If you love the sweetness of dried fruit, you'll find this breakfast dish to die for. If you have a really sweet tooth, you can make it even more delicious by drizzling over a little clear honey before serving. Be careful not to overdo it, though, as this may ruin the taste of the fruit.

VARIATIONS You can use any dried fruit for this dish – choose whichever you like best.

poached eggs florentine

Ingredients | SERVES 4

675g | 1½lb spinach, washed and drained

25g | 1oz | 2 tbsp butter

60ml | 4 tbsp double (heavy) cream

pinch of freshly grated nutmeg

salt and ground black pepper

4 eggs

shavings of Gruyère or Parmesan cheese,
to garnish (optional)

FOR THE SAUCE

25g | 1oz | 2 tbsp butter

25g | 1oz | ¼ cup plain (all-purpose) flour

300ml | ½ pint | 1¼ cups hot milk

pinch of ground mace

115g | 4oz | 1 cup grated Gruyère cheese

1 Preheat the oven to 200°C | 400°F | Gas 6. Place the spinach in a large pan with a little water. Cook for about 3–4 minutes, then drain well and chop finely. Return the spinach to the pan and add the butter, cream, nutmeg and seasoning. Heat until warmed through, then spoon into four small ovenproof dishes, making a well in the middle of each.

2 To make the topping, heat the butter in a small pan, add the flour and cook for about 1 minute, stirring. Gradually blend in the hot milk, beating well. Cook for another 2 minutes, stirring constantly. Remove from the heat, and stir in the mace and 75g | 3oz | ¾ cup of the Gruyère cheese.

3 Break each egg into a cup and slide it into a pan of lightly salted simmering water. Poach for 3–4 minutes. Lift out the eggs using a slotted spoon and drain on kitchen paper. Place a poached egg in the middle of each dish and cover with the cheese sauce.

4 Place in the oven and bake for 10 minutes or until just golden. Serve immediately, garnished with a few shavings of Gruyère or Parmesan cheese, if using.

VARIATIONS Although not technically Florentine, this dish can be prepared with any other green vegetable that is in season, such as chard, fennel or Chinese leaves (Chinese cabbage).

"Florentine" dishes, which are cooked in the "style of Florence", always contain spinach and may also be topped with a creamy cheese sauce. This recipe combines both, as well as lightly poached eggs, to make a delicious brunch dish. It may be a little rich for children, but if you have guests staying then this dish will impress.

eggs benedict

This traditional dish, consisting of a poached egg, laid on a ham-topped English muffin and then coated with hollandaise sauce, is the perfect dish for a relaxed Sunday brunch – especially if it's in bed. Best of all, it only takes minutes to make. After all no one wants to spend too much time in the kitchen on a Sunday morning.

Ingredients | SERVES 4

4 eggs

2 English muffins or 4 slices of bread

butter, for spreading

4 thick slices cooked ham, cut to fit the muffins

fresh chives, to garnish

FOR THE SAUCE

3 egg yolks

30ml | 2 tbsp fresh lemon juice

1.5ml | 1/4 tsp salt

115g | 4oz | 1/2 cup butter

30ml | 2 tbsp single (light) cream

ground black pepper

COOK'S TIP
Use only very fresh eggs for poaching, because they keep their shape better in the water.

1 To make the sauce, blend the egg yolks, lemon juice and salt in a food processor or blender for no more than 15 seconds.

2 Melt the butter in a small pan until it bubbles, but do not let it brown. With the motor running, carefully pour the hot butter into the food processor or blender through the feed tube in a slow, steady stream. Turn off the machine as soon as all the butter has been added.

3 Pour the sauce into a bowl, placed over a pan of simmering water. Stir for 2–3 minutes, until thickened. If the sauce begins to curdle, whisk in 15ml | 1 tbsp boiling water. Stir in the cream and season with pepper. Remove the pan from the heat, leaving the bowl on top to keep the sauce warm.

4 Bring a shallow pan of lightly salted water to the boil. Break each egg into a cup, then slide it carefully into the water. Delicately turn the white around the yolk with a spoon. Poach for 3–4 minutes until the white is set. Remove the eggs from the pan, one at a time, using a slotted spoon, and drain on kitchen paper. Cut off any ragged edges with a small knife or scissors.

5 While the eggs are poaching, split and toast the muffins or toast the slices of bread. Spread with butter while still warm.

6 Place a piece of ham, which you may brown in butter if you wish, on each muffin half or slice of toast, then place a poached egg on each one. Spoon the warm sauce over the eggs, garnish with chives and serve.

bagels

These ring-shaped rolls were created by a Jewish baker from Vienna in the 17th century. The dough is first poached to give it a chewy texture and then baked. Served topped with cream cheese and smoked salmon, these bagels are a delicious and quite luxurious breakfast treat – even more so if eaten on a weekday.

Ingredients | MAKES 10-12

7g packet easy-blend (rapid-rise) dried yeast

25ml | 1½ tbsp salt

500g | 1¼lb | 4½ cups strong white bread flour, plus extra for dusting

250ml | 8fl oz | 1 cup lukewarm water

oil, for greasing

3-4 litres | 5-7 pints water

30ml | 2 tbsp sugar

corn meal, for sprinkling

1 egg yolk

VARIATIONS Add dried onions, garlic granules or poppy seeds to the bagel dough before shaping or top the bagels with poppy seeds, sesame seeds, caraway seeds, dried onion or garlic granules before baking.

1 In a bowl, combine the yeast, salt and flour. Pour the lukewarm water into a separate large bowl. Gradually add half the flour to the lukewarm water, beating until it forms a smooth, soft batter. Knead the remaining flour into the batter until the mixture forms a fairly firm, smooth dough.

2 On a lightly floured surface, knead the dough for 10–20 minutes or, if using a bread machine, 5–8 minutes, until shiny and smooth. If the dough is sticky, add a little more flour. (The dough should be much firmer than ordinary bread dough.)

3 Lightly oil a bowl. Place the dough in it and turn to coat it completely in oil. Cover with a clean dishtowel and leave in a warm place for about 40 minutes, or until doubled in size.

4 Turn the dough on to a lightly floured surface and knock down with your fist. Knead for 3–4 minutes, until smooth and elastic. Divide into 10–12 balls. Poke your thumb through each one, open the hole and form a bagel measuring 6–7.5cm | 2½–3in in diameter. Place on a floured board to rise for 20 minutes.

5 Preheat the oven to 200°C | 400°F | Gas 6. Boil the water in a large pan, add the sugar, then lower to a gentle boil. Lightly oil a baking sheet and sprinkle with corn meal. Beat the egg yolk with 15ml | 1 tbsp water. Add the bagels to the boiling water in a single layer, and poach for 8 minutes, turning occasionally. Remove, drain and place on the prepared baking sheet. Brush with the egg mixture. Bake for 25–30 minutes, until well browned. Cool on a wire rack.

SOUPS AND LIGHT MEALS

Eggs, fish and shellfish are perfect for soups and light meals and this chapter includes innovative serving suggestions. Try poached eggs in a tasty garlic soup or with a stylish salad. Zesty lime enlivens scallops and bright samphire, while a classic terrine of haddock and smoked salmon provides a taste of tradition.

seafood soup noodles

Ingredients | SERVES 6

175g|6oz tiger prawns (jumbo shrimp), peeled and deveined

225g|8oz monkfish fillet, cut into chunks

225g|8oz salmon fillet, cut into chunks

5ml|1 tsp vegetable oil

15ml|1 tbsp dry white wine

225g|8oz|2 cups dried egg vermicelli

1.2 litres|2 pints|5 cups fish stock

1 carrot, thinly sliced

225g|8oz asparagus, cut into 5cm|2in lengths

30ml|2 tbsp dark soy sauce

5ml|1 tsp sesame oil

salt and ground black pepper

2 spring onions (scallions), cut into thin rings, to garnish

Lightly poached prawns, monkfish and fresh salmon give this Chinese soup a superb flavour. Sounds of enjoyment are a compliment to the Chinese cook, so slurping it is not only permissible, but desirable.

1 Mix the prawns and fish in a bowl. Add the vegetable oil and wine with 1.5ml|¼ tsp salt and a little black pepper. Mix together lightly, cover and marinate in a cool place for about 15 minutes.

2 Bring a large pan of water to the boil, add the noodles and cook for 4 minutes until just tender, or according to the instructions on the packet. Drain the noodles thoroughly and divide among six serving bowls. Cover the bowls to keep the noodles warm.

3 Bring the fish stock to the boil in a large pan. Add the prawns and monkfish, poach for 1 minute, add the salmon and poach for 2 minutes more.

4 Using a slotted spoon, lift the fish and prawns out of the stock, add to the noodles in the bowls and keep hot.

5 Strain the stock through a sieve lined with muslin (cheesecloth) into a clean pan. Bring to the boil and poach the carrot slices and asparagus for about 2 minutes, then add the soy sauce and sesame oil, with salt to taste. Stir well.

6 Pour the stock and vegetables over the noodles and seafood, garnish with the spring onions and serve.

VARIATION Try this simple recipe using rice vermicelli for a slightly different texture and taste.

garlic and coriander soup

Ingredients | SERVES 6

25g|1oz fresh coriander (cilantro),
leaves and stalks chopped separately

1.5 litres|2½ pints|6¼ cups vegetable or
chicken stock, or water

5–6 plump garlic cloves

5ml|1 tsp salt

6 eggs

275g|10oz day-old bread, most of the crust
removed, torn into bitesize pieces

90ml|6 tbsp extra virgin olive oil,
plus extra to serve

salt and ground black pepper

1 Place only the coriander stalks in a large pan. Add the stock or water and bring to the boil. Simmer for 10 minutes, then process in a blender or food processor and press through a sieve (strainer) back into the pan.

2 Chop the garlic with 5ml|1 tsp salt, then stir in 120ml|4fl oz|½ cup of the hot soup. Return the mixture to the pan.

3 Slide the eggs into a frying pan of simmering water (adding one at a time) and poach for about 3–4 minutes, until just set. Use a slotted spoon to remove them from the pan and transfer to a warmed plate. Using a small knife or scissors, trim off any untidy bits of white.

4 Bring the soup back to the boil and add seasoning. Stir in the chopped coriander leaves and remove the pan from the heat.

5 Place the bread in six soup plates or bowls and drizzle the oil over it. Ladle-in the soup and stir. Add a poached egg to each bowl and serve immediately, offering olive oil at the table so that it can be drizzled over the soup to taste.

COOK'S TIP It is important that you add the poached egg only to soup that is to be served immediately. If you plan to serve only two bowls of soup, then poach only two eggs. The remaining soup (without egg) can be refrigerated.

This recipe is based on the bread soups of Portugal. Being a simple soup it should be made with the best ingredients – plump, juicy garlic, fragrant coriander, and wholesome, thick chunks of country bread. A freshly poached egg is finally added to each serving to make this a delicious light meal in itself.

warm dressed salad with poached eggs

Ingredients | SERVES 2

½ small loaf Granary (whole-wheat) bread

45ml|3 tbsp chilli oil

2 eggs

115g|4oz mixed salad leaves

45ml|3 tbsp extra virgin olive oil

2 garlic cloves, crushed

15ml|1 tbsp balsamic or sherry vinegar

50g|2oz|½ cup Parmesan cheese, shaved

ground black pepper (optional)

Soft, lightly poached eggs, hot chilli-flavoured croûtons and cool, crisp salad leaves make a lively and unusual combination. This delicious salad is perfect to serve for a summer lunch.

1 Carefully cut the crust from the Granary loaf and discard it. Cut the bread into 2.5cm|1in cubes.

2 Heat the chilli oil in a large frying pan. Add the bread cubes and cook for about 5 minutes, tossing the cubes occasionally, until they are crisp

3 Meanwhile, bring a pan of water to the boil. Break each egg into a jug (pitcher) or cup and slide into the water. Poach for 4 minutes, until lightly cooked.

4 Divide the salad leaves between two plates. Arrange the croûtons on top.

5 Wipe the frying pan clean with kitchen paper. Heat the olive oil in the pan, add the garlic and vinegar and cook over a high heat for 1 minute. Pour the warm dressing over the salads.

6 Place a poached egg on each salad and top with thin Parmesan shavings and a little freshly ground black pepper, if you like.

VARIATION If you would prefer to make the dish less spicy, cook the croûtons in olive oil or a nut oil, such as walnut or hazelnut, rather than using chilli oil.

skate with bitter salad leaves

Skate has a deliciously sweet flavour which contrasts well with the bitterness of salad leaves such as escarole, lamb's lettuce, frisée and radicchio and the tang of orange zest. This dish is perfect for a light, healthy supper. The recipe serves four, but it is easy to make for a larger number: simply double or treble the quantities, depending on how many people you need to feed.

Ingredients | SERVES 4

800g | 1³/₄lb skate wings

15ml | 1 tbsp white wine vinegar

4 black peppercorns

1 fresh thyme sprig

175g | 6oz mixed bitter salad leaves, such as frisée, rocket (arugula), radicchio, escarole and lamb's lettuce

1 orange

2 tomatoes, peeled, seeded and diced

warm French bread, to serve

FOR THE DRESSING

15ml | 1 tbsp white wine vinegar

45ml | 3 tbsp olive oil

2 shallots, finely chopped

salt and ground black pepper

1 Put the skate wings into a large shallow pan, cover with cold water and add the vinegar, peppercorns and thyme. Bring to the boil, then poach the fish gently for about 8–10 minutes, until the flesh of the fish comes away easily from the bones.

2 Meanwhile, make the dressing. Whisk the vinegar, olive oil and shallots together in a bowl. Season with salt and pepper to taste. Place the salad leaves in a serving bowl, pour over the dressing and toss well.

3 Using a zester, remove the outer rind from the orange and set aside. Peel the orange, removing all the pith, and slice into thin rounds.

4 When the skate is cooked, flake the flesh and mix it into the salad. Add the orange rind shreds, the orange slices and tomatoes and toss gently. Serve with the warmed, French bread.

COOK'S TIP To peel tomatoes easily, cut a cross in the top and plunge them briefly into a bowl of hot water.

scallops with samphire and lime

1 Wash the samphire in several changes of cold water. Drain, then trim off any woody ends. Bring a pan of water to the boil, then drop in the samphire and cook for 3–5 minutes. Drain, refresh under cold water and drain again. Set aside.

2 If the scallops are large, cut them in half horizontally. Detach the corals. In a shallow pan, bring the wine to the boil and cook until it is reduced by about one-third. Lower the heat and add the lime juice to the pan.

3 Add the scallops and corals and poach gently for 3–4 minutes until the scallops are just cooked, but still opaque. Remove and set aside.

4 Leave the cooking liquid to cool until tepid, then whisk in the groundnut or vegetable oil. Add the samphire, cucumber, scallops and corals and toss lightly to mix.

5 Grind some black pepper over the mixture, cover and leave at room temperature for about 1 hour; this will allow the flavours to develop. Divide the mixture among four individual dishes and then garnish with the chopped fresh parsley. Serve the dish at room temperature.

COOK'S TIP Samphire grows wild in estuaries and salt marshes in Europe and North America. High-quality fishmongers sometimes stock it.

Ingredients | SERVES 4

225g|8oz fresh samphire

12 large (sea) or 24 queen (baby) scallops, out of the shell

300ml|1/2 pint|1 1/4 cups dry white wine

juice of 2 limes

15ml|1 tbsp groundnut (peanut) or vegetable oil

1/2 cucumber, seeded and diced

black pepper, for grinding

chopped fresh parsley, to garnish

Samphire, also known as rock samphire, is a herb with a wonderful taste and aroma of the sea. For this reason it is the perfect complement to seafood dishes. The green samphire, and the colourful poached corals of the scallops ensure that this dish looks fabulous as well as tasting delicious.

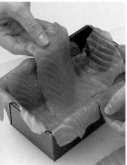

haddock and smoked salmon terrine

Like many traditional recipes, the terrine is named after the receptacle in which it is made. It looks impressive and makes a superb dish for a summer meal or as part of a buffet.

Ingredients | SERVES 6–8

15ml|1 tbsp sunflower oil, for greasing

350g|12oz oak-smoked salmon

900g|2lb haddock fillets, skinned

2 eggs, lightly beaten

105ml|7 tbsp sour cream

30ml|2 tbsp drained bottled capers

30ml|2 tbsp drained soft green or pink peppercorns

salt and ground white pepper

sour cream, peppercorns and fresh dill and rocket (arugula), to garnish

COOK'S TIP For the best flavour and nutritional value, use organic or wild salmon rather than the cheaper farmed variety.

1 Preheat the oven to 200°C|400°F| Gas 6. Grease a 1 litre|1³/₄ pint|4 cup loaf tin (pan) or terrine. Use some of the salmon to line the tin; let some of the ends overhang the edges. Reserve the remaining smoked salmon.

2 Cut two slices of haddock the length of the tin and set aside. Cut the rest into small pieces. Season all the haddock with salt and pepper.

3 Combine the eggs, sour cream, capers and peppercorns in a bowl. Season, then stir in the pieces of haddock. Spoon half the mixture into the tin. Smooth the surface with a spatula.

4 Wrap the long haddock fillets in the reserved smoked salmon. Lay the wrapped haddock fillets on top of the fish mixture in the tin.

5 Fill the tin with the remaining fish mixture, smooth the surface and fold over the overhanging pieces of smoked salmon. Cover with foil.

6 Tap the tin to settle the contents, then stand it in a roasting pan and pour boiling water halfway up the sides. Bake for 45–60 minutes until the filling is just set.

7 Remove from the roasting pan, but do not remove the foil cover. Place three heavy cans on the foil and leave until cold. Refrigerate for 24 hours.

8 About 1 hour before serving, remove the weights and the foil. Carefully invert on to a serving plate and lift off the tin. Cut into thick slices and serve, garnished with sour cream, peppercorns, dill and rocket leaves.

quenelles of sole

Traditionally, these light fish "dumplings" are made with pike, but they taste even better when made with sole or other types of white fish. When poaching the quenelles, it is important to keep the heat low so that they hold their shape – if the water becomes too hot, they may disintegrate.

Ingredients | SERVES 6

450g|1lb sole fillets, skinned and cut into large pieces

4 egg whites

600ml|1 pint|2¹/₂ cups double (heavy) cream

salt, black pepper
and grated nutmeg

chopped fresh parsley, to garnish

FOR THE SAUCE

1 small shallot, finely chopped

60ml|4 tbsp dry vermouth, such as Noilly Prat

120ml|4fl oz|¹/₂ cup fish stock

150ml|¹/₄ pint|²/₃ cup double (heavy) cream

50g|2oz|¹/₄ cup butter, chilled and diced

COOK'S TIP These dumplings are rich yet delicate in flavour, so they are best accompanied by simple vegetables such as plain boiled potatoes or steamed broccoli.

1 Remove any bones from the sole, place in a blender or food processor and season generously. Switch on the blender and while the motor is running add the egg whites, one at a time, through the feeder tube to make a smooth purée. Using the back of a spoon, press the purée through a metal sieve placed over a bowl. Stand the bowl of purée in a larger bowl and surround it with plenty of crushed ice or ice cubes.

2 Whip the cream until very thick and floppy, but not stiff. Gradually fold it into the fish mousse, making sure each spoonful has been absorbed completely before adding the next. Season with salt and pepper, then stir in nutmeg to taste. Cover the bowl of mousse and chill (still in its bowl of ice) for several hours.

3 To make the sauce, combine the shallot, vermouth and stock in a small pan. Bring to the boil and cook until reduced by half. Add the cream and boil until the consistency of thin cream. Strain, return to the pan and whisk in the butter, one piece at a time, until creamy. Season, and keep warm.

4 Bring a wide, shallow pan of lightly salted water to the boil; reduce the heat so the water barely trembles. Using two tablespoons dipped in hot water, shape the mousse into ovals. Slip them into the simmering water.

5 Poach in batches for 8–10 minutes, until they feel just firm to the touch. As each is cooked, remove, drain on kitchen paper and keep hot. Arrange on heated plates, pour the sauce around and serve garnished with the parsley.

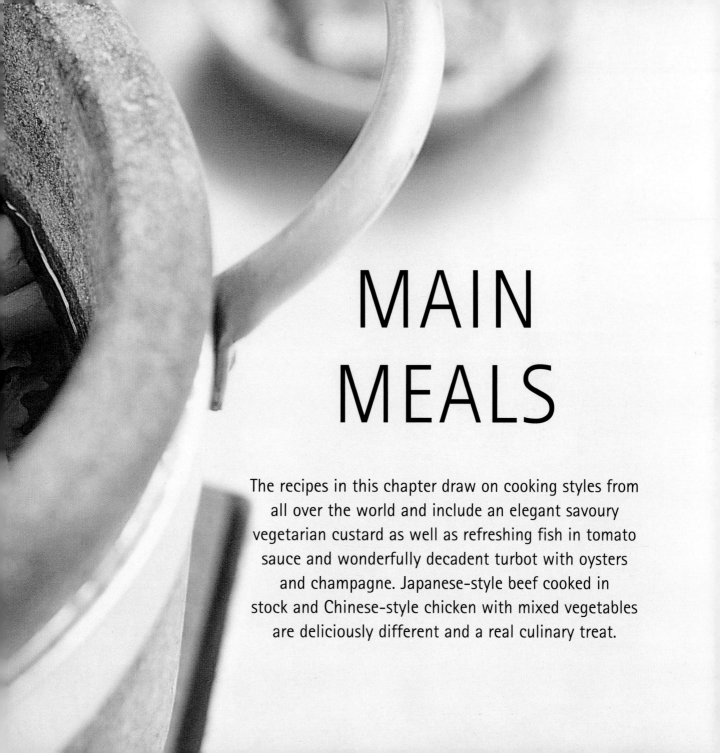

MAIN MEALS

The recipes in this chapter draw on cooking styles from all over the world and include an elegant savoury vegetarian custard as well as refreshing fish in tomato sauce and wonderfully decadent turbot with oysters and champagne. Japanese-style beef cooked in stock and Chinese-style chicken with mixed vegetables are deliciously different and a real culinary treat.

roasted garlic and aubergine custards with red pepper

These elegant little custards are made in ramekin dishes and then poached in a bain-marie. They make a rather splendid vegetarian main course for a special dinner.

Ingredients | SERVES 6

2 large garlic heads

6–7 fresh thyme sprigs

60ml|4 tbsp extra virgin olive oil, plus extra for greasing

350g|12oz aubergines (eggplant), cut into 1cm|1/2in dice

2 large red (bell) peppers, halved and seeded

pinch of saffron strands

300ml|1/2 pint|1 1/4 cups whipping cream

2 large (US extra large) eggs

pinch of caster (superfine) sugar

30ml|2 tbsp shredded fresh basil leaves

salt and ground black pepper

FOR THE DRESSING

90ml|6 tbsp extra virgin olive oil

15–25ml|1–1 1/2 tbsp balsamic vinegar

pinch of caster (superfine) sugar

115g|4oz tomatoes, peeled, seeded and diced

1/2 small red onion, finely chopped

generous pinch of ground toasted cumin seeds

handful of fresh basil leaves

1 Preheat the oven to 190°C|375°F| Gas 5. Place the garlic on a piece of foil with the thyme and sprinkle with 15ml|1 tbsp of the oil. Wrap in the foil and bake for 40 minutes. Remove and cool slightly. Reduce the oven temperature to 180°C|350°F|Gas 4.

2 Heat the remaining oil in a heavy pan. Add the aubergines and fry for 6–8 minutes. Remove from the pan, set aside and retain the oil. Grill (broil) the peppers, skin sides up, until black. Place in a bowl, cover and leave for 10 minutes. When cooled, skin and dice them. Soak the saffron in 15ml|1 tbsp hot water for 10 minutes. Pop the garlic from its skin, discard the thyme and foil. Blend in a food processor, adding the retained oil, the cream, eggs and saffron, with its liquid. Season. Add sugar, half the diced pepper and basil.

3 Lightly oil 6 large ovenproof ramekins (about 200–250ml|7–8fl oz| 1 cup capacity) and line with circles of baking parchment. Oil the paper. Divide the aubergines among the dishes. Pour over the egg mixture, then place in a roasting pan. Cover each dish with foil and make a little hole in the centre. Pour hot water into the pan, halfway up the sides of the ramekins. Bake for 25–30 minutes.

4 For the dressing, whisk the oil and vinegar with salt, pepper and a pinch of sugar. Stir in the tomatoes, onion, remaining red pepper and cumin. Set aside some basil leaves for garnishing; chop the rest and add to the dressing.

5 Leave the custards to cool for 5 minutes, then turn out. Pour dressing around them, and garnish with basil.

poached fish in spicy tomato herb sauce

Ingredients | SERVES 8

60ml|4 tbsp chopped fresh parsley

1 large onion

60ml|4 tbsp chopped fresh coriander (cilantro) leaves

fresh chilli or chilli paste, to taste

5–8 garlic cloves, crushed

300ml|1/2 pint|1 1/4 cups passata (bottled strained tomatoes)

150ml|1/4 pint|2/3 cup fish stock

large pinch of ground ginger

large pinch of curry powder

1.5ml|1/4 tsp ground cumin

1.5ml|1/4 tsp ground turmeric

seeds from 2–3 cardamom pods

juice of 2 lemons, plus extra if needed

30ml|2 tbsp vegetable or olive oil

1.5kg|3 1/4lb mixed white fish fillets

salt and ground black pepper

warm pitta breads, to serve

This simple dish of delicately flavoured poached white fish is enlivened with a spicy sauce to make it a real family favourite. Mixed white fish is suggested but the dish is just as good using only one type of fish, such as cod or flounder.

1 Chop the onion, parsley, coriander and fresh chilli. Crush the garlic.

2 Put the passata, stock, onion, herbs, garlic, chilli, ginger, curry powder, cumin, turmeric, cardamom, lemon juice and oil into a pan and bring to the boil.

3 Remove the pan from the heat and add the fish fillets to the hot sauce.

4 Return to the heat and allow the sauce to boil briefly again. Reduce the heat and poach the fish very gently for about 5 minutes, or until tender.

5 Taste the sauce and adjust the seasoning, adding more lemon juice if necessary. Divide between individual serving plates and serve with the warmed pitta breads to mop up the spicy tomato sauce.

fillets of turbot with oysters

This luxurious dish is perfect for special occasions or a small dinner party. It is worth buying a whole turbot and asking the fishmonger to fillet and skin it for you – don't be embarrassed to ask, that's what fishmongers are for. Keep the head, bones and trimmings for stock. Sole, brill and halibut can all be substituted for the turbot.

Ingredients | SERVES 4

12 Pacific (rock) oysters

115g|4oz|1/2 cup butter

2 carrots, cut into julienne strips

200g|7oz celeriac, cut into julienne strips

the white parts of 2 leeks, cut into julienne strips

375ml|13fl oz|generous 1 1/2 cups champagne or dry white sparkling wine (about 1/2 bottle)

105ml|7 tbsp whipping cream

1 turbot, about 1.75kg|3–3 1/2lb, cut into 4 fillets and skinned

salt and ground white pepper

1 Using an oyster knife, open the oysters over a bowl to make sure that you catch the juices. Remove from their shells and place in a separate bowl. Set aside. Discard the shells.

2 Melt 25g|1oz|2 tbsp of the butter in a shallow pan, add the vegetable julienne and cook over a low heat until tender but not coloured. Pour in half the champagne and cook gently until the liquid has evaporated, ensuring that the vegetables do not colour.

3 Strain the oyster juices into a small pan and add the cream and the remaining champagne. Stir over a medium heat until the consistency of thin cream. Dice half the remaining butter and whisk in, a little at a time, until smooth. Season, then pour into a blender and whizz until velvety smooth.

4 Return the sauce to the pan, bring to just below boiling point, then drop in the oysters. Poach for about 1 minute, to warm but barely cook the oysters. Keep warm, but do not let the sauce boil.

5 Season the turbot fillets with salt and pepper. Heat the remaining butter in a large frying pan until foaming, then fry the fillets over a medium heat for about 2–3 minutes on each side until cooked through and golden in colour.

6 Cut each turbot fillet into three pieces and arrange on individual warmed plates. Pile the vegetable julienne on top, place three oysters around the turbot fillets on each plate and pour the sauce around the edge. Serve immediately.

Chinese-style chicken with mixed vegetables

Ingredients | SERVES 4

350g|12oz skinless chicken breast fillets

20ml|4 tsp vegetable oil

1.5ml|¼ tsp salt

300ml|½ pint|1¼ cups chicken stock

75g|3oz|¾ cup drained, canned
straw mushrooms

50g|2oz|½ cup drained, sliced canned
bamboo shoots

50g|2oz|⅓ cup drained, canned
water chestnuts, sliced

1 small carrot, sliced

50g|2oz|½ cup mangetouts (snow peas)

15ml|1 tbsp dry sherry

15ml|1 tbsp oyster sauce

5ml|1 tsp caster (superfine) sugar

5ml|1 tsp cornflour (cornstarch)

15ml|1 tbsp cold water

salt and white pepper

Fillets of chicken poached in chicken stock are both succulent and tender. With the addition of crisp vegetables, this delectable Chinese dish is a riot of colour and has plenty of contrasts in terms of texture and taste to make a complete and nutritious meal.

1 Put the chicken in a shallow bowl. Add 5ml|1 tsp of the oil, 1.5ml|¼ tsp salt, and a generous pinch of pepper. Cover and set aside for 10 minutes.

2 Bring the stock to the boil in a pan. Add the chicken and poach for 12 minutes, or until tender. Drain and slice, reserving 75ml|5 tbsp of the stock.

3 Heat the remaining oil in a non-stick frying pan or wok. Add all the vegetables and stir-fry for 2 minutes.

4 Add the sherry, oyster sauce, caster sugar and reserved stock to the vegetables and stir well. Stir in the chicken and then cook for a further 2 minutes.

5 Mix the cornflour with the cold water until it forms a paste. Add the mixture to the pan and cook, stirring the sauce until it begins to thicken slightly. Season the mixture to taste with salt and white pepper and then serve immediately.

VARIATIONS Other suitable vegetables include beansprouts, baby corn, broccoli or cauliflower florets, shelled peas and diced (bell) peppers; use whatever combination you prefer, making sure you have a good balance of flavours.

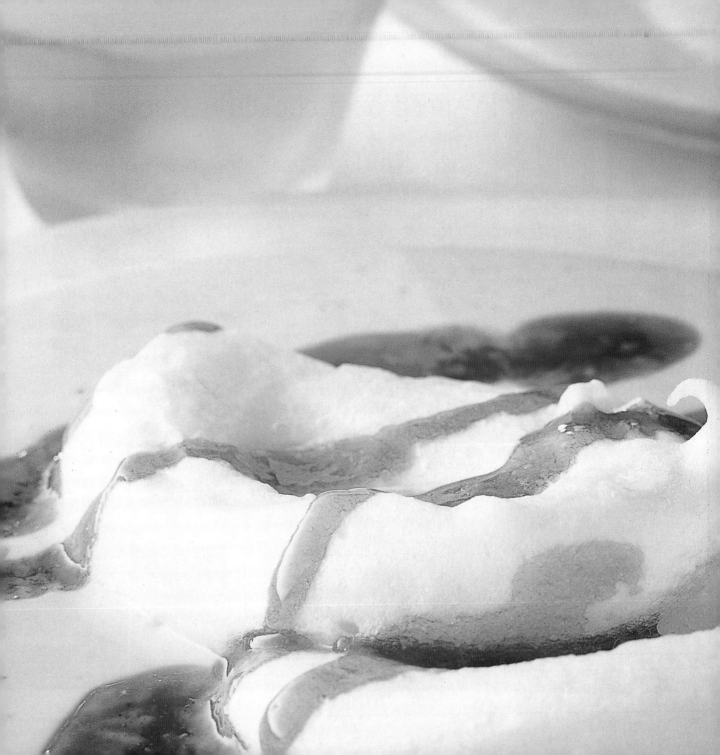

paper-thin sliced beef cooked in stock

Ingredients | SERVES 4

600g|1lb 5oz boneless beef sirloin

2 thin leeks, trimmed and cut into thick strips

4 spring onions (scallions), quartered

8 shiitake mushrooms, stalks removed

175g|6oz oyster mushrooms, chopped

1/2 Chinese cabbage, cut into small squares

300g|11oz shungiku, (chrysanthemum leaves), halved

275g|10oz tofu, diced

10 x 6cm|4 x 2 1/2 in dried kelp

FOR THE CITRUS SAUCE

juice of 1 lime with 1/2 cup of lemon juice

50ml|2fl oz|1/4 cup rice vinegar

120ml|4fl oz|1/2 cup soy sauce

20ml|4 tsp rice wine

4 x 6cm|1 1/2 x 2 1/2 in dried kelp

5g|1/8 oz dried tuna flakes

FOR THE SESAME SAUCE

75g|3oz white sesame seeds

10ml|2 tsp caster (superfine) sugar

45ml|3 tbsp shoyu

30ml|2 tbsp rice wine

90ml|6 tbsp fish stock

20 chives, finely chopped

FOR THE CONDIMENTS

5–6cm|2–2 1/2 in mooli (daikon), peeled

2 dried chillies, seeded and sliced

You will find the more unusual ingredients for this Japanese dish, known as Shabu Shabu, in Japanese supermarkets. You will also need a portable stove to cook this dish at the table.

1 Mix all the citrus sauce ingredients in a glass jar and leave overnight. Strain and keep the liquid in the jar.

2 Make the sesame sauce. Roast the sesame seeds in a dry frying pan on a low heat until they pop. Grind to form a smooth paste. Grind in the sugar, then mix in the shoyu, wine and stock. Pour 30ml|2 tbsp into each of four small bowls, and divide the chives among them. Put the rest of the sauce in a bowl.

3 Prepare the condiments. Pierce the cut ends of the mooli deeply 4–5 times with a skewer, then insert pieces of chilli. Leave for 20 minutes. Finely grate (shred) the mooli into a sieve (strainer). Divide among four bowls.

4 Cut the meat into paper-thin slices, and place on a serving plate. Place the vegetables and tofu on another plate.

5 Fill a flameproof casserole three-quarters full of water and add the dried kelp. Heat the casserole. Pour 45ml|3 tbsp citrus sauce into the mooli bowls. When the water comes to the boil, remove the dried kelp and reduce the heat to medium-low. Add a handful of each ingredient except the beef to the casserole.

6 Hold the beef in the stock for 3–10 seconds. Then dip the beef in the other sauces and eat. The vegetables and tofu can be eaten as they cook.

DESSERTS

Poached meringues in that irresistible dessert called "floating islands" and creamy coconut custards feature here, as well as a wonderful array of fruit desserts. Mulled in wine, spiked with exotic ginger and star anise, coated in chocolate fudge sauce or wrapped in crêpes, poached fruit has never tasted so good.

winter fruit poached in mulled wine

Ingredients | SERVES 4

300ml|1/2 pint|1 1/4 cups red wine

300ml|1/2 pint|1 1/4 cups fresh orange juice

finely grated rind and juice of 1 orange

45ml|3 tbsp clear honey or barley malt syrup

1 cinnamon stick, broken in half

4 cloves

4 cardamom pods, split

2 pears, such as Comice or Williams, peeled, cored and halved

8 ready-to-eat dried figs

12 ready-to-eat dried apricots

2 eating apples, peeled, cored and thickly sliced

Fresh apples and pears are combined with dried apricots and figs to create a spicy cocktail. This simple dessert, warming and rich, is the perfect choice for serving in winter.

1 Put the wine, the fresh and squeezed orange juice and half the orange rind in a pan with the honey or syrup and spices. Bring to the boil, then reduce the heat and simmer for about 2 minutes, stirring occasionally.

2 Add the pears, figs and apricots and poach, covered, for about 25 minutes, occasionally turning the fruit in the wine. Add the sliced apples and poach for a further 12–15 minutes until the fruit is soft and tender.

3 Using a slotted spoon, carefully remove the fruit from the pan. Put the fruit into a serving bowl and keep warm. Discard the spices.

4 Cook the wine mixture over a high heat until it has reduced and become syrupy, then pour it over the fruit.

5 Serve the fruit hot. If you wish to add some decoration you can sprinkle over some of the reserved orange rind.

VARIATION You can replace some of the fruit with your own personal favourite and serve with either crème fraîche or yogurt to make the dessert even tastier.

pears with ginger and star anise

Ingredients | SERVES 4

75g|3oz|6 tbsp caster (superfine) sugar

300ml|1/2 pint|1 1/4 cups white dessert wine

thinly pared rind and juice of 1 lemon

7.5cm|3in piece of fresh root ginger, peeled and bruised

5 star anise

10 cloves

600ml|1 pint|2 1/2 cups cold water

6 slightly unripe pears

25g|1oz|3 tbsp drained, preserved stem ginger in syrup, sliced

natural (plain) yogurt or fromage frais, to serve

The addition of star anise and ginger gives a refreshing twist to these poached pears, and as the dish can be prepared in advance, it is ideal for entertaining.

1 Place the caster sugar, dessert wine, lemon rind and juice, fresh root ginger, star anise, cloves and water into a pan just large enough to hold all the pears together in a snug position. Bring to the boil.

2 Meanwhile, peel the pears, leaving the stems intact. Add them to the wine mixture, making sure that they are totally immersed in the liquid. Return the wine mixture to the boil, lower the heat, cover and poach for 15–20 minutes or until the pears are tender.

3 Lift out the pears with a slotted spoon and place them in a heatproof dish. Boil the wine syrup rapidly until it is reduced by about half, then pour over the pears. Allow them to cool, then chill.

4 Cut the pears into thick slices and arrange on four serving plates. Remove the ginger and whole spices from the wine sauce, stir in the preserved ginger and spoon the sauce over the pears. Serve with the natural yogurt or fromage frais.

COOK'S TIP When buying the pears for this recipe make sure that they are not quite ripe. If the pears are too soft they will become mushy when cooked; if under-ripe they may be too hard, but should become tender if cooked for long enough.

pears in chocolate fudge blankets

Ingredients | SERVES 6

6 ripe eating pears

30ml|2 tbsp lemon juice

75g|3oz|1/3 cup caster (superfine) sugar

300ml|1/2 pint|1 1/4 cups water

1 cinnamon stick

FOR THE SAUCE

200ml|7fl oz|scant 1 cup double (heavy) cream

150g|5oz|scant 1 cup light muscovado (brown) sugar

25g|1oz|2 tbsp unsalted (sweet) butter

60ml|4 tbsp golden (light corn) syrup

120ml|4fl oz|1/2 cup milk

200g|7oz dark (bittersweet) chocolate, broken into squares

1 Peel the pears, leaving the stalks on. Scoop out the cores from the base. Brush the cut surfaces with lemon juice to prevent browning.

2 Place the sugar and water in a large pan. Heat gently until the sugar dissolves. Add the pears and cinnamon stick with any remaining lemon juice and, if necessary, a little more water, so that the pears are almost covered. Bring to the boil, then lower the heat, cover the pan and poach the pears gently for 15–20 minutes, or until they are just tender.

3 Meanwhile, make the sauce. Place the cream, sugar, butter, golden syrup and milk in a heavy pan.

4 Heat gently, stirring, until the sugar has dissolved and the butter and syrup have melted, then bring to the boil. Boil, stirring constantly, for about 5 minutes or until the sauce is thick and smooth. Remove from the heat and stir in the chocolate, a few squares at a time, until melted.

5 Using a slotted spoon, transfer the poached pears to a dish. Keep hot. Boil the syrup rapidly to reduce to about 45–60ml|3–4 tbsp. Remove the cinnamon stick and stir the syrup into the chocolate sauce.

6 Serve the pears on individual plates, with the hot chocolate fudge sauce spooned over.

The delicate flavour of pears is exquisitely enhanced by poaching in a spiced syrup, and the combination with chocolate is a marriage made in heaven. It's no wonder that this simple, classic dish is such an enduring favourite – it's not difficult to make, but luxurious enough for the most elegant dinner party.

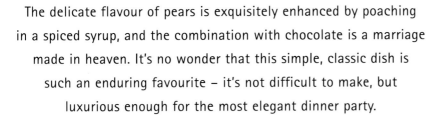

chocolate crêpes with poached plums and port

A good dinner party dessert, this dish always looks impressive. You can use different fruits, such as cherries or orange segments, and replace the port with a fruit liqueur if you like.

Ingredients | SERVES 5-6

50g|2oz dark (bittersweet) chocolate, broken into squares

200ml|7fl oz|scant 1 cup milk

120ml|4fl oz|½ cup single (light) cream

30ml|2 tbsp cocoa powder (unsweetened)

115g|4oz|1 cup plain (all-purpose) flour

2 eggs

FOR THE FILLING

500g|1¼lb red or golden plums

50g|2oz|¼ cup caster (superfine) sugar

30ml|2 tbsp water

30ml|2 tbsp port

oil, for frying

175g|6oz|¾ cup crème fraîche

FOR THE SAUCE

150g|5oz dark (bittersweet) chocolate, broken into squares

175ml|6fl oz|¾ cup double (heavy) cream

30ml|2 tbsp port

1 Place the chocolate in a pan with the milk. Heat gently until the chocolate has melted.

2 Pour the chocolate sauce into a blender or food processor and add the cream, cocoa powder, flour and eggs. Process until smooth, then pour into a jug (pitcher) and chill in the refrigerator for about 30 minutes.

3 Meanwhile, make the filling. Halve and stone (pit) the plums. Place them in a pan and add the sugar and water.

4 Bring to the boil, then lower the heat. Cover, and poach the plums for about 10 minutes or until they are tender. Stir in the port; poach for a further 30 seconds. Remove the pan from the heat, keeping the lid on to make sure they stay warm.

5 Have ready a sheet of baking parchment. Heat a crêpe pan, grease it lightly with a little oil, then pour in just enough batter to cover the base of the pan, swirling to coat evenly. Cook until the crêpe has set, then flip it over to cook the other side. Slide the crêpe out on to the sheet of parchment, then cook 9 to 11 more crêpes in the same way.

6 Make the sauce. Combine the chocolate and cream in a pan. Heat gently, stirring until the sauce is smooth. Add the port and heat gently, stirring, for 1 minute.

7 Divide the plum filling between the crêpes, add a dollop of crème fraîche to each and roll them up carefully. Serve in individual bowls, with the chocolate sauce spooned over the top.

floating islands

The French name for this dish is *Oeufs à la Neige*, meaning "snow eggs". Traditionally the meringues are poached in milk; however, this method uses water for poaching, which gives a lighter result. The delicate texture of meringue works wonderfully well with creamy custard and a drizzling of caramel.

Ingredients | SERVES 4-6

1 vanilla pod (bean)
600ml|1 pint|2½ cups milk
8 egg yolks
50g|2oz|¼ cup granulated sugar

FOR THE MERINGUES
4 large (US extra large) egg whites
1.5ml|¼ tsp cream of tartar
225g|8oz|1¼ cups caster (superfine) sugar

FOR THE CARAMEL
150g|5oz|¾ cup granulated sugar
45ml|3 tbsp water

COOK'S TIPS
Do not make the caramel too far ahead or it will soften the meringues as it sits on top of them. If you do not have a vanilla pod, you can use 5ml|1 tsp vanilla essence (extract) instead.

1 Split the vanilla pod lengthways and scrape the seeds into a pan. Add the milk and vanilla pod and bring to the boil, stirring frequently. Remove from heat and cover. Leave for 20 minutes.

2 Whisk the egg yolks and sugar together for 2–3 minutes until thick and creamy. Remove the vanilla pod from the milk, then whisk into the egg mixture and return to the pan.

3 Stir the sauce over a medium-low heat until it begins to thicken and coats the back of a spoon. Strain into a chilled bowl, allow to cool, stirring occasionally, then chill until needed.

4 Half-fill a large frying pan with water and bring just to simmering point. In a clean, grease-free bowl, whisk the egg whites slowly until they are frothy.

5 Add the cream of tartar, increase the speed of whisking and continue until soft peaks are formed. Sprinkle over the caster sugar, about 30ml|2 tbsp at a time. Whisk until stiff and glossy.

6 Using two tablespoons, form egg-shaped meringues and slide into the water (you may need to work in batches). Poach for 3 minutes, turning once, until just firm. Use a slotted spoon to transfer the meringues to a baking sheet lined with kitchen paper. Pour the custard into serving dishes and arrange the meringues on top.

7 To make the caramel, put the sugar into a small pan with 45ml|3 tbsp of water. Bring to the boil, swirling until dissolved, then boil until the syrup turns a dark colour. Drizzle over the meringues and custard and serve cold.

coconut custards

Ingredients | SERVES 4

4 eggs

75g|3oz|6 tbsp soft light brown sugar

250ml|8fl oz|1 cup coconut milk

5ml|1 tsp vanilla essence (extract), rose water or jasmine water

fresh mint leaves and icing (confectioners') sugar, to decorate

sliced fruit, to serve

This traditional dessert is poached in the oven and is often served with sweet sticky rice and a selection of fresh fruit. Mangoes and papaya go particularly well with the custard and rice.

1 Preheat the oven to 150°C|300°F|Gas 2. Whisk the eggs and sugar in a bowl until smooth. Add the coconut milk and flavouring, and whisk well.

2 Strain the mixture into a jug (pitcher), then pour it into four individual heatproof glasses, ramekins or an ovenproof dish.

3 Stand the glasses, ramekins or dish in a roasting pan. Fill the pan with hot water to reach halfway up the sides of the glasses, ramekins or dish.

4 Place in the oven and cook for about 35–40 minutes, or until the custards are set. You can test this by inserting a fine skewer or cocktail stick (toothpick) into the custard.

5 Remove the roasting pan from the oven, lift out the glasses, ramekins or dish and leave to cool.

6 If you like, turn out each custard on to a serving plate. Decorate with the mint leaves and a dusting of icing sugar, and serve with sliced fruit.

COOK'S TIP If you are making these delicious custards for guests, it is easier to prepare them a day in advance and keep them in the refrigerator until needed.